Success With

Multiplication Facts

SCHOLASTIC

Editor: Ourania Papacharalambous
Cover design by Tannaz Fassihi; cover illustration by Kevin Zimmer
Interior design by Cynthia Ng
Interior illustrations by Rusty Fletcher (5, 15); Doug Jones (7, 10, 18, 20, 22–24, 28, 30, 35), Mike Moran (31, 45); Cynthia Ng (14, 41, 43); Pauline Reeves (21)

ISBN 978-1-338-79855-5
Scholastic Inc., 557 Broadway, New York, NY 10012
Copyright © 2022 Scholastic Inc.
All rights reserved. Printed in the U.S.A.
First printing, January 2022
1 2 3 4 5 6 7 8 9 10   40 29 28 27 26 25 24 23 22

INTRODUCTION

Parents and teachers alike will find *Scholastic Success With Multiplication Facts* to be a valuable resource. Students will enjoy completing a wide variety of engaging activities as they sharpen their skills with multiplication facts. On page 4, you will find a list of the key skills covered in the activities throughout this book. Remember to praise students for their efforts and successes!

TABLE OF CONTENTS

Grade-Appropriate Skills Covered in *Scholastic Success With Multiplication Facts: Grades 3–4*

Interpret products of whole numbers, e.g., interpret 5 × 7 as the total number of objects in 5 groups of 7 objects each.

Use multiplication and division within 100 to solve word problems in situations involving equal groups, arrays, and measurement quantities.

Determine the unknown whole number in a multiplication or division equation relating three whole numbers.

Apply properties of operations as strategies to multiply and divide.

Fluently multiply and divide within 100, using strategies such as the relationship between multiplication and division or properties of operations.

Solve two-step word problems using the four operations. Represent these problems using equations with a letter standing for the unknown quantity. Assess the reasonableness of answers using mental computation and estimation strategies including rounding.

Multiply one-digit whole numbers by multiples of 10 in the range 10-90 using strategies based on place value and properties of operations.

Interpret a multiplication equation as a comparison.

Multiply or divide to solve word problems involving multiplicative comparison.

Generate a number or shape pattern that follows a given rule.

Recognize that in a multi-digit whole number, a digit in one place represents ten times what it represents in the place to its right.

A Ray of Fun

An **array** demonstrates a multiplication sentence. The first **factor** tells how many rows there are. The second **factor** tells how many there are in each row. The answer to a multiplication sentence is called the **product**.

2 × 4 = 8   ○○○○   2 rows
○○○○   4 in each row

Write the multiplication sentence for each array.

1 ○○○
○○○

_____

2 ○○○
○○○
○○○

_____

3 ○○
○○
○○
○○

_____

4 ○○○○○
○○○○○
○○○○○

_____

5 ○○○

_____

6 ○○○○
○○○○
○○○○
○○○○

_____

7 ○○○○○○
○○○○○○

_____

8 ○○○○
○○○○
○○○○

_____

9 ○○○○○○
○○○○○○
○○○○○○

_____

10 ○○○
○○○
○○○
○○○
○○○

_____

11 ○
○
○
○
○

_____

12 ○○
○○
○○
○○
○○
○○
○○

_____

13 ○○
○○
○○

_____

14 ○○○○
○○○○

_____

15 ○○○○○○○
○○○○○○○
○○○○○○○
○○○○○○○

_____

16 ○○○○○
○○○○○
○○○○○

_____

Time to Group

The multiplication symbol (×) can be thought of as meaning "groups of."

3 "groups of " 4 equals 12
3 × 4 = 12

5 "groups of " 2 equals 10
5 × 2 = 10

Write the multiplication sentence for each diagram.

1

2

3

4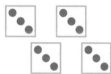

_____

_____

_____

_____

5

6

7

8

_____

_____

_____

_____

9

10

11

12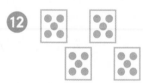

_____

_____

_____

_____

13

14

15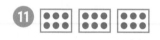

16

_____

_____

_____

_____

 William has 5 bags of oranges. There are 7 oranges in each bag.
On another sheet of paper, draw a diagram to show the total number of
oranges. Then, write a multiplication sentence.

Adding Quickly

Write a multiplication sentence
for each addition sentence.

The addition sentence
4 + 4 + 4 + 4 + 4 = 20 can be
written as a multiplication sentence.
Count how many times 4 is being
added together. The answer is 5.
So, 4 + 4 + 4 + 4 + 4 = 20 can be
written as 5 × 4 = 20. Multiplication
is a quick way to add.

1 5 + 5 + 5 = 15

_____

2 6 + 6 + 6 + 6 = 24

_____

3 8 + 8 = 16

_____

4 2 + 2 + 2 + 2 = 8

_____

5 7 + 7 + 7 = 21

_____

6 4 + 4 + 4 + 4 = 16

_____

7 9 + 9 + 9 = 27

_____

8 5 + 5 + 5 + 5 + 5 = 25

_____

9 3 + 3 + 3 + 3 + 3 = 15

_____

10 10 + 10 + 10 + 10 = 40

_____

11 1 + 1 + 1 + 1 + 1 = 5

_____

12 11 + 11 + 11 = 33

_____

13 8 + 8 + 8 + 8 = 32

_____

14 0 + 0 + 0 + 0 = 0

_____

15 12 + 12 + 12 + 12 = 48

_____

16 9 + 9 + 9 + 9 = 36

_____

What's My Line?

5 × 3 = 15 can be demonstrated on a number line.

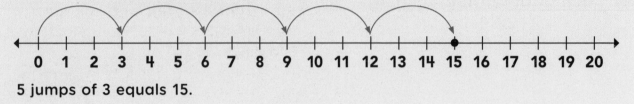

5 jumps of 3 equals 15.

Write the multiplication sentence demonstrated on each number line.

1 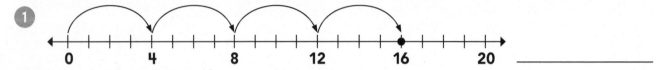 _____

2 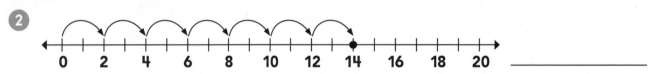 _____

3 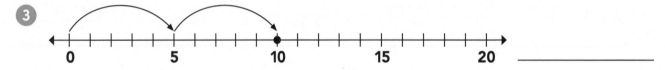 _____

4 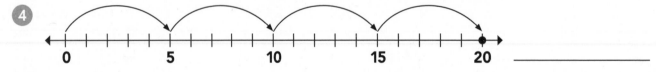 _____

5 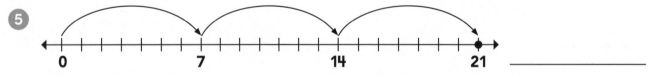 _____

6 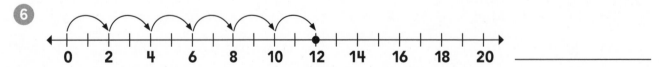 _____

7 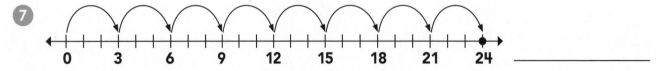 _____

8 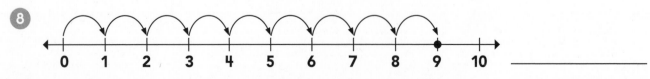 _____

Change It Up

Change the order of the factors in each multiplication sentence.

The order of the factors in a multiplication sentence can change without changing the value of the product. If 2 × 7 is changed to 7 × 2, the product still equals 14.

1 6 × 2 = 12

_____

2 3 × 9 = 27

_____

3 5 × 9 = 45

_____

4 7 × 4 = 28

_____

5 9 × 8 = 72

_____

6 4 × 10 = 40

_____

7 2 × 11 = 22

_____

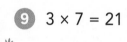

8 4 × 8 = 32

_____

9 3 × 7 = 21

_____

10 6 × 7 = 42

_____

11 3 × 12 = 36

_____

12 6 × 5 = 30

_____

13 9 × 7 = 63

_____

14 12 × 11 = 132

_____

Family Fun

Multiplication is the opposite of division. The product and factors can be used to write division sentences. The multiplication and division sentences are called a **fact family**.

$2 \times 6 = 12$ (2 groups of 6) $12 \div 6 = 2$ (12 divided into 6 equal groups)
$6 \times 2 = 12$ (6 groups of 2) $12 \div 2 = 6$ (12 divided into 2 equal groups)

Write two multiplication and two division sentences for each set of numbers.

1 2, 3, 6

_____

_____

_____

_____

2 3, 5, 15

_____

_____

_____

_____

3 5, 6, 30

_____

_____

_____

_____

4 2, 8, 16

_____

_____

_____

_____

5 3, 9, 27

_____

_____

_____

_____

6 6, 7, 42

_____

_____

_____

_____

7 4, 5, 20

_____

_____

_____

_____

8 8, 5, 40

_____

_____

_____

_____

9 4, 8, 32

_____

_____

_____

_____

Jay has 33 marbles. There are an equal number of marbles in each of 3 bags. On another sheet of paper, write a number sentence to figure out how many marbles are in each bag. Then, write the set of numbers in this fact family.

Grid and Count It

A multiplication sentence can be diagrammed on a **coordinate grid**. To show 5 × 4, use the factors as the ordered pair (5, 4). Then, go over 5 and up 4 on the grid, and mark the point where the lines intersect to make a rectangle. Finally, count all the squares in the rectangle.

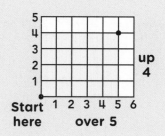

First, write the ordered pair for each set of multiplication factors. Then, mark the intersecting point for the ordered pair on the grid. Color and count each square in the rectangle. Fill in the blank with the total number of squares that are in the rectangle.

1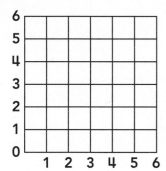

3 × 4 = (   )

Total Squares = _____

2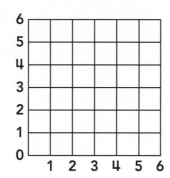

2 × 4 = (   )

Total Squares = _____

3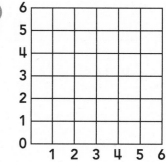

3 × 2 = (   )

Total Squares = _____

4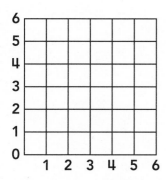

1 × 5 = (   )

Total Squares = _____

5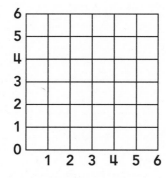

5 × 2 = (   )

Total Squares = _____

6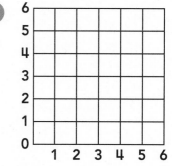

3 × 6 = (   )

Total Squares = _____

Find the Patterns

What is the pattern for the numbers 0, 2, 4, 6, 8, 10, 12, 14, 16, 18? The pattern shows multiples of 2.

Complete each pattern.

1. 3, 6, 9, 12, _____, _____, _____, _____, _____

2. 4, 8, 12, 16, _____, _____, _____, _____, _____

3. 1, 2, 3, 4, _____, _____, _____, _____, _____

4. 7, 14, 21, _____, _____, _____, _____, _____

5. 10, 20, 30, _____, _____, _____, _____, _____

6. _____, 18, 27, _____, _____, _____, _____

7. 6, 12, _____, _____, 30, _____, _____, _____

8. _____, 22, _____, 44, _____, _____, _____, 88

9. 5, 10, 15, _____, _____, _____, _____, _____

10. 8, _____, 24, _____, 40, _____, _____, _____

11. 10, 12, 14, _____, _____, _____, 22, _____, _____

12. _____, 24, _____, 48, 60, _____, _____, _____, _____

Code Zero!
Code One!

Multiply. Shade all products of 0 yellow.
Shade all other products green.

When a number is multiplied by 0, the product is always 0. When a number is multiplied by 1, the product is always the number being multiplied.

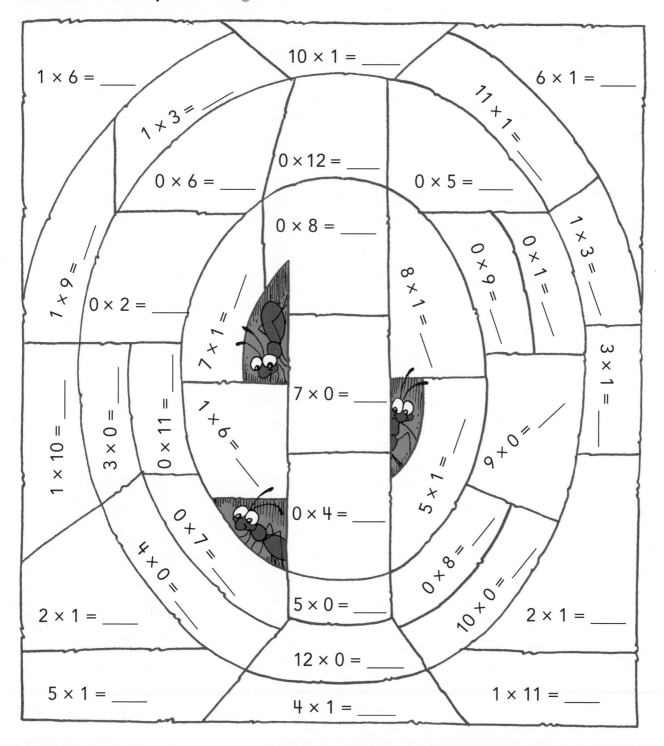

$1 \times 6 =$ _____

$10 \times 1 =$ _____

$6 \times 1 =$ _____

$1 \times 3 =$ _____

$11 \times 1 =$ _____

$0 \times 6 =$ _____

$0 \times 12 =$ _____

$0 \times 5 =$ _____

$0 \times 8 =$ _____

$1 \times 9 =$ _____

$0 \times 2 =$ _____

$0 \times 9 =$ _____

$0 \times 1 =$ _____

$1 \times 3 =$ _____

$7 \times 1 =$ _____

$8 \times 1 =$ _____

$3 \times 1 =$ _____

$7 \times 0 =$ _____

$1 \times 10 =$ _____

$3 \times 0 =$ _____

$0 \times 11 =$ _____

$1 \times 6 =$ _____

$9 \times 0 =$ _____

$5 \times 1 =$ _____

$0 \times 7 =$ _____

$0 \times 4 =$ _____

$4 \times 0 =$ _____

$0 \times 8 =$ _____

$2 \times 1 =$ _____

$5 \times 0 =$ _____

$10 \times 0 =$ _____

$2 \times 1 =$ _____

$12 \times 0 =$ _____

$5 \times 1 =$ _____

$4 \times 1 =$ _____

$1 \times 11 =$ _____

Two, Four, Six, Eight, Who Do We Appreciate?

When multiplying by 2, skip count by 2, or think of number line jumping!

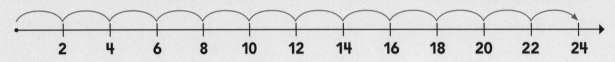

Multiply.

1 2 × 3 = _____   2 × 8 = _____   11 × 2 = _____   2 × 7 = _____

2 8 × 2 = _____   4 × 2 = _____   2 × 2 = _____   2 × 4 = _____

3 12 × 2 = _____   5 × 2 = _____   10 × 2 = _____   2 × 12 = _____

4 9 × 2 = _____   2 × 1 = _____   2 × 10 = _____   7 × 2 = _____

5 2 × 0 = _____   2 × 6 = _____   3 × 2 = _____   0 × 2 = _____

6 2 × 5 = _____   2 × 9 = _____

7 6 × 2 = _____   1 × 2 = _____

8 2 × 11 = _____   2 × 2 = _____

On another sheet of paper, write a rhyme to go with each multiplication fact for 2. Examples: "2 × 4 = 8, I love math, can you relate?" Or, "2 × 4 = 8, I've got to go, and shut the gate!"

Aim for the Stars

Color each cloud with a correct multiplication sentence to show the path to the moon.

2 × 3 = 6

12 × 2 = 24

6 × 2 = 8

2 × 9 = 11

8 × 2 = 16

1 × 2 = 1

4 × 2 = 8

2 × 7 = 14

11 × 2 = 22

2 × 5 = 10

2 × 6 = 12

3 × 2 = 5

2 × 8 = 14

7 × 2 = 12

2 × 10 = 20

2 × 2 = 4

2 × 12 = 26

9 × 2 = 18

2 × 1 = 2

The Three Factory

Multiply.

START →

$3 \times 12 =$ _____

$3 \times 4 =$ _____

$3 \times 9 =$ _____

$3 \times 0 =$ _____

$9 \times 3 =$ _____

$6 \times 3 =$ _____

$2 \times 3 =$ _____

$8 \times 3 =$ _____

$4 \times 3 =$ _____

$5 \times 3 =$ _____

$3 \times 3 =$ _____

$3 \times 1 =$ _____

$3 \times 10 =$ _____

$3 \times 6 =$ _____

OK

$12 \times 3 =$ _____

$3 \times 8 =$ _____

$1 \times 3 =$ _____

$7 \times 3 =$ _____

$3 \times 5 =$ _____

$10 \times 3 =$ _____

$3 \times 11 =$ _____

$0 \times 3 =$ _____

$3 \times 4 =$ _____

$6 \times 3 =$ _____

$8 \times 3 =$ _____

$3 \times 12 =$ _____

$3 \times 3 =$ _____

$3 \times 7 =$ _____

$3 \times 2 =$ _____

$10 \times 3 =$ _____

$3 \times 9 =$ _____

$11 \times 3 =$ _____

A Positive Answer

What should you say if you are asked, "Do you want to learn the 3s?"

To find out, look at each problem below. If the product is correct, color the space green. If the product is incorrect, color the space yellow.

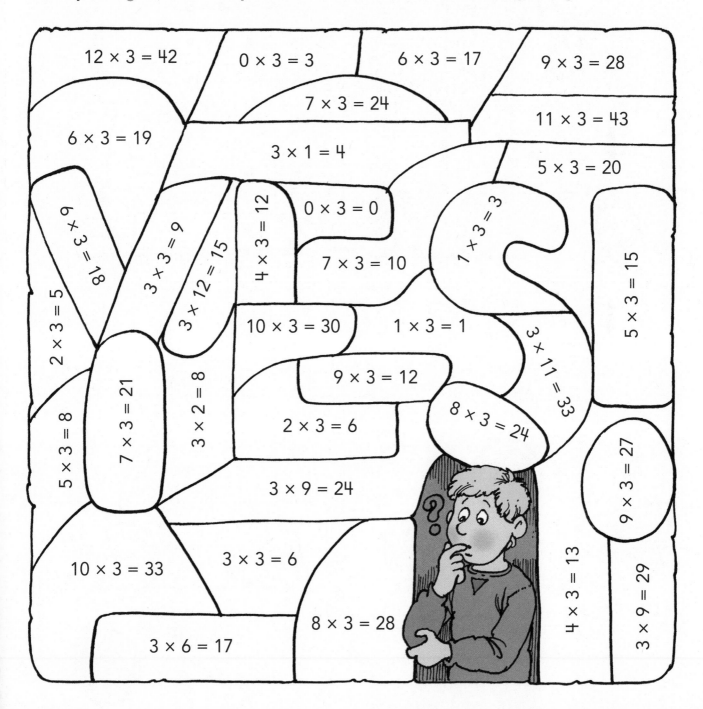

12 × 3 = 42

0 × 3 = 3

6 × 3 = 17

9 × 3 = 28

7 × 3 = 24

11 × 3 = 43

6 × 3 = 19

3 × 1 = 4

5 × 3 = 20

6 × 3 = 18

3 × 3 = 9

3 × 12 = 15

4 × 3 = 12

0 × 3 = 0

1 × 3 = 3

5 × 3 = 15

7 × 3 = 10

2 × 3 = 5

10 × 3 = 30

1 × 3 = 1

3 × 11 = 33

5 × 3 = 8

7 × 3 = 21

3 × 2 = 8

9 × 3 = 12

8 × 3 = 24

9 × 3 = 27

2 × 3 = 6

3 × 9 = 24

10 × 3 = 33

3 × 3 = 6

4 × 3 = 13

3 × 9 = 29

8 × 3 = 28

3 × 6 = 17

Puzzling Facts

Multiply. Write the number word for each product in the puzzle. Don't forget the hyphens! The first one is done for you.

Across

3. 4 × 9 = __36__

4. 4 × 5 = _____

7. 4 × 3 = _____

8. 4 × 7 = _____

9. 4 × 10 = _____

11. 4 × 0 = _____

12. 4 × 11 = _____

Down

1. 4 × 4 = _____

2. 4 × 12 = _____

5. 4 × 2 = _____

6. 4 × 6 = _____

10. 4 × 1 = _____

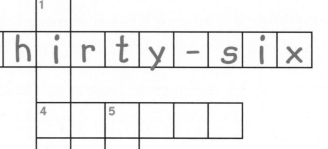

t h i r t y - s i x

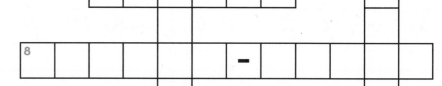

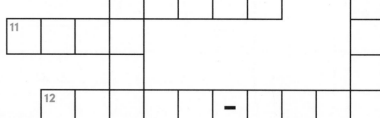

 Tracy was missing 4 buttons on 11 different shirts. How many buttons does she need to fix all the shirts? Show your work on another sheet of paper.

Fantastic Four

Don't you just adore the factor 4?

To answer this question, multiply. Then, use the code to write the letter of each multiplication sentence on the blank above its product.

A 4 × 10 =   I 4 × 0 =   O 4 × 7 =   T 4 × 8 =

D 4 × 4 =   M 4 × 2 =   R 4 × 6 =   Y 4 × 9 =

E 4 × 11 =   N 4 × 5 =   S 4 × 3 =   ! 4 × 12 =

| 36 | 44 | 12 | 48 | | 0 | | 40 | 16 | 28 | 24 | 44 | | 0 | 32 |

| 8 | 28 | 24 | 44 | | 40 | 20 | 16 | | 8 | 28 | 24 | 44 | 48 |

 On another sheet of paper, write a message to a friend. Make a code using the multiplication facts for 4. Have your friend use the code to read the message.

We Can Make Fives Come Alive and Thrive!

What letter stands for "math" and "multiplication"?

To find out, complete each problem. Connect the dots in order from least to greatest.

$5 \times 2 =$

$5 \times 4 =$

_____

_____

$5 \times 1 =$ ●

●

●

● $5 \times 5 =$

_____

_____

$5 \times 11 =$

$5 \times 8 =$

_____

_____

●

●

●

$5 \times 3 =$

_____

$5 \times 10 =$

$5 \times 9 =$

_____

_____

$5 \times 0 =$ ●———————●

●

●

●

● $5 \times 6 =$

$5 \times 12 =$

$5 \times 7 =$

_____

_____

_____

_____

 There are 5 children in line to buy ice cream cones. If each child buys a cone with 3 scoops of ice cream, how many total scoops of ice cream will the store sell? Show your work on another sheet of paper.

How Many Can You Find?

Complete each multiplication sentence. Then, circle each answer in the picture.

1. $2 \times 5 = $ _____

2. $5 \times $ _____ $= 5$

3. _____ $\times 5 = 35$

4. $10 \times 5 = $ _____

5. _____ $\times 5 = 60$

6. $5 \times 6 = $ _____

7. _____ $\times 5 = 55$

8. $5 \times 3 = $ _____

9. $8 \times 5 = $ _____

10. _____ $\times 5 = 45$

11. $2 \times $ _____ $= 10$

12. _____ $\times 5 = 25$

13. $7 \times 5 = $ _____

14. $5 \times 12 = $ _____

15. $5 \times $ _____ $= 20$

 Squeaky Squirrel lived in a tree with 4 squirrel friends. If each squirrel collected 12 nuts, how many nuts in all did the squirrels collect? Show your work on another sheet of paper.

Scholastic Success With Multiplication Facts • Grades 3–4

Follow the Path

Multiply. Then, follow the path from each multiplication sentence to its product.

Let's review! The multiplication symbol (×) means "groups of."

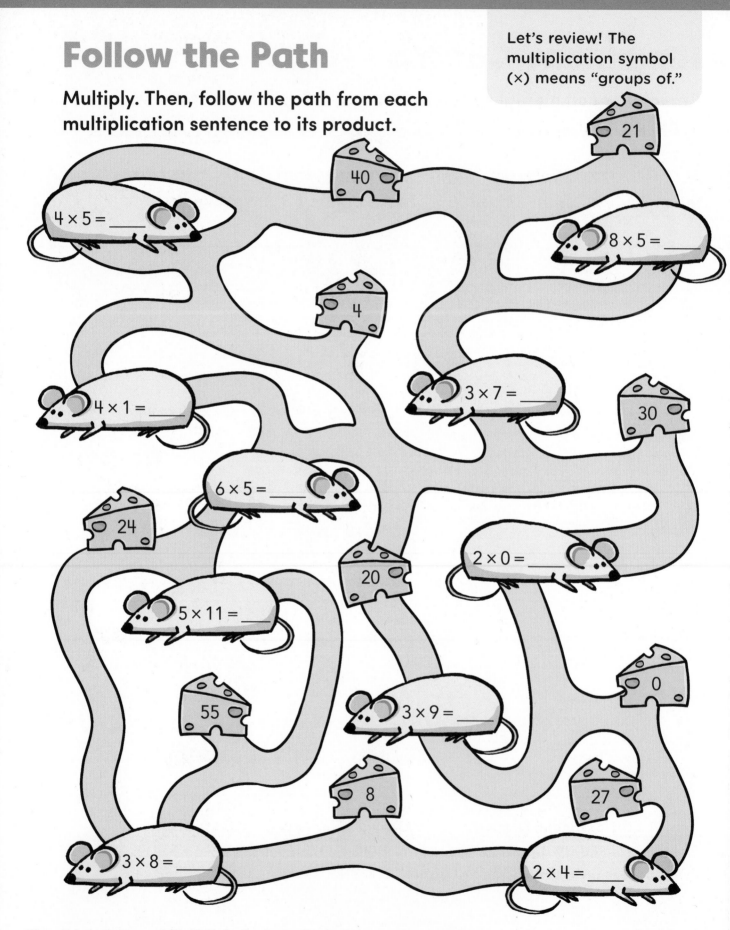

$4 \times 5 =$ _____

$8 \times 5 =$ _____

21

40

4

$4 \times 1 =$ _____

$3 \times 7 =$ _____

30

$6 \times 5 =$ _____

24

$2 \times 0 =$ _____

20

$5 \times 11 =$ _____

0

55

$3 \times 9 =$ _____

$3 \times 8 =$ _____

8

27

$2 \times 4 =$ _____

Riddle and Review

Why did the teacher choose multiplication to help his class grow?

Let's review some more! The numbers being multiplied are called **factors**. The answer is called the **product**.

To find out, multiply. Use the code to write the letter of each multiplication sentence on the blank above its product.

A 3 × 12 =   H 2 × 9 =   O 3 × 7 =   U 2 × 12 =

B 5 × 10 =   I 4 × 7 =   P 1 × 0 =   W 5 × 5 =

D 2 × 8 =   L 5 × 6 =   R 2 × 11 =   Y 4 × 12 =

E 4 × 11 =   M 4 × 8 =   S 5 × 7 =   ! 3 × 3 =

G 2 × 6 =   N 3 × 9 =   T 5 × 9 =

__ __   __ __ __ __   __ __ __   __ __ __ __ __
35 21   45 18 36 45   18 28 35   12 22 21 24 0

__ __ __ __ __   __ __ __ __ __   __ __   __ __ __
25 21 24 30 16   50 44 12 28 27   45 21   12 44 45

__ __ __ __ __ __   __ __ __
30 36 22 12 44 22   36 27 16

• Factors

• Products

__ __ __ __ __ __ __ __ __
32 24 30 45 28 0 30 48 9

On a field trip to the Science Museum, Mr. Weaver divided his class into 6 groups. Ms. Vega divided her class into 5 groups. Each group had 4 students. How many students are in each class? Which class has more students? Solve the problem on another sheet of paper.

Quality Math

How can you be sure that multiplication is quality math?

To find out, multiply. Then, use the code to write the letter of each multiplication sentence on the blank above its product.

A 2 × 11 =   G 4 × 4 =   P 5 × 8 =   V 3 × 11 =

B 1 × 7 =   H 5 × 12 =   R 5 × 6 =   Y 3 × 8 =

C 2 × 9 =   I 2 × 6 =   S 5 × 9 =   ! 5 × 0 =

D 4 × 12 =   M 4 × 11 =   T 5 × 7 =

E 4 × 9 =   O 3 × 7 =   U 4 × 7 =

$\overline{7}$ $\overline{36}$ $\overline{18}$ $\overline{22}$ $\overline{28}$ $\overline{45}$ $\overline{36}$ $\overline{24}$ $\overline{21}$ $\overline{28}$ $\overline{60}$ $\overline{22}$ $\overline{33}$ $\overline{36}$

$\overline{35}$ $\overline{60}$ $\overline{36}$ $\overline{30}$ $\overline{12}$ $\overline{16}$ $\overline{60}$ $\overline{35}$ $\overline{40}$ $\overline{30}$ $\overline{21}$ $\overline{48}$ $\overline{28}$ $\overline{18}$ $\overline{35}$

$\overline{36}$ $\overline{33}$ $\overline{36}$ $\overline{30}$ $\overline{24}$ $\overline{35}$ $\overline{12}$ $\overline{44}$ $\overline{36}$ $\overline{0}$

CHIPS

Brand X

Quality Math

Brand Y

Mathematics Fireworks

Multiply. On another sheet of paper, find the sum of the products of each star trail. Then, use the key to color each star to match its star trail sum.

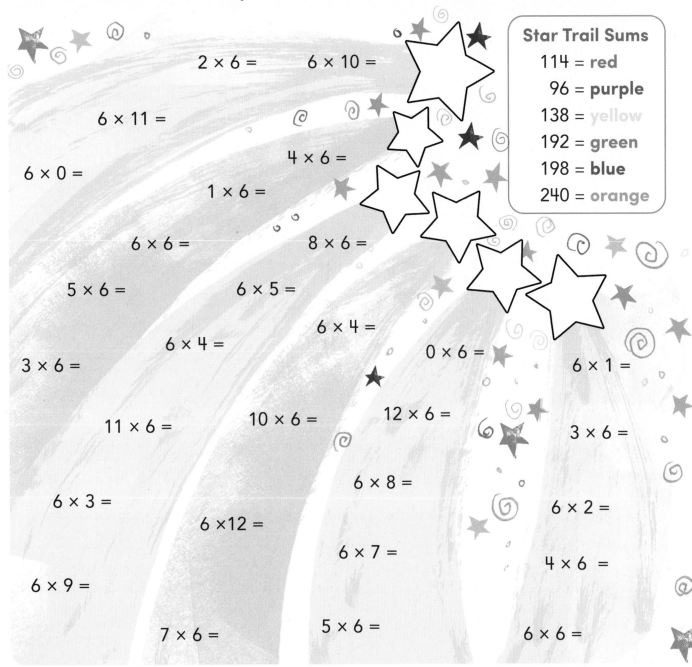

Star Trail Sums
114 = red
96 = purple
138 = yellow
192 = green
198 = blue
240 = orange

$2 \times 6 =$ $6 \times 10 =$

$6 \times 11 =$

$6 \times 0 =$ $4 \times 6 =$
                     $1 \times 6 =$

$6 \times 6 =$ $8 \times 6 =$

$5 \times 6 =$ $6 \times 5 =$

$6 \times 4 =$ $6 \times 4 =$

$3 \times 6 =$ $0 \times 6 =$ $6 \times 1 =$

$11 \times 6 =$ $10 \times 6 =$ $12 \times 6 =$ $3 \times 6 =$

$6 \times 3 =$ $6 \times 8 =$

$6 \times 12 =$ $6 \times 2 =$

$6 \times 7 =$

$6 \times 9 =$ $4 \times 6 =$

$7 \times 6 =$ $5 \times 6 =$ $6 \times 6 =$

 On the Fourth of July, Emma counted 6 different fireworks every 15 minutes. The show lasted 2 hours. How many fireworks did she see? Show your work on another sheet of paper.

Can You Crack the Code?

| 0 | 1 | 2 | 3 | 4 | 5 | 6 | 7 | 8 | 9 | 10 | 11 | 12 |

Using the above key, write a multiplication sentence for each message.

1. ☁ × ⬡ = ◯ ▲ _____

2. ⬡ × ★ = ☁ ✹ _____

3. ❀ × ⬡ = ★ ▱ _____

4. ♥ × ⬡ = ◯ ⬡ _____

5. ⬡ × ■ = ◯ ■ _____

6. ▱ × ⬡ = ■ ▱ _____

7. ▲ × ⬡ = ▱ ▲ _____

8. ◆ × ⬡ = ▱ ■ _____

9. ⬡ × ✚ = ◆ ■ _____

10. ✹ × ⬡ = ✹ _____

11. ◯ × ⬡ = ⬡ _____

12. ☾ × ⬡ = ⬡ ✹ _____

· ·

Multiply. Then, write each multiplication sentence in code.
Use the above key.

1. 5 × 6 = ____   _____

2. 6 × 7 = ____   _____

3. 6 × 9 = ____   _____

4. 6 × 3 = ____   _____

5. 6 × 8 = ____   _____

6. 6 × 6 = ____   _____

7. 12 × 6 = ____   _____

8. 6 × 10 = ____   _____

Abby wrote the same message to 6 different friends. She made a code using flower symbols for each of the 12 letters in her message. How many total flower symbols did she write? Show your work on another sheet of paper.

The "Seven" Statues

Multiply.

$7 \times 2 = $ _____

$1 \times 7 = $ _____

$8 \times 7 = $ _____

$12 \times 7 = $ _____

$7 \times 5 = $ _____

$7 \times 9 = $ _____

$7 \times 10 = $ _____

$0 \times 7 = $ _____

$7 \times 11 = $ _____

$7 \times 12 = $ _____

$7 \times 7 = $ _____

$7 \times 8 = $ _____

$3 \times 7 = $ _____

$9 \times 7 = $ _____

$7 \times 4 = $ _____

$11 \times 7 = $ _____

$6 \times 7 = $ _____

Maurice was hired to build 7 statues in front of City Hall. He calculated that each statue would take him 6 months to finish. The statues need to be completed before the music festival that is scheduled to take place in exactly 2 years. How many months will it take Maurice to complete the statues? Will Maurice have enough time? Show your work on another sheet of paper.

Flying Sevens

Multiply.

$1 \times 7 =$ _____

$7 \times 11 =$ _____

$7 \times 9 =$ _____

$11 \times 7 =$ _____

$3 \times 7 =$ _____

$6 \times 7 =$ _____

$7 \times 7 =$ _____

$7 \times 10 =$ _____

$0 \times 7 =$ _____

$7 \times 4 =$ _____

$7 \times 8 =$ _____

$2 \times 7 =$ _____

$7 \times 1 =$ _____

$5 \times 7 =$ _____

$7 \times 12 =$ _____

$7 \times 2 =$ _____

$4 \times 7 =$ _____

$7 \times 6 =$ _____

$8 \times 7 =$ _____

$7 \times 3 =$ _____

$7 \times 5 =$ _____

$12 \times 7 =$ _____

$9 \times 7 =$ _____

$7 \times 0 =$ _____

$10 \times 7 =$ _____

The Ultimate Eight Track

Use a stopwatch to time how long it takes to multiply around the track.

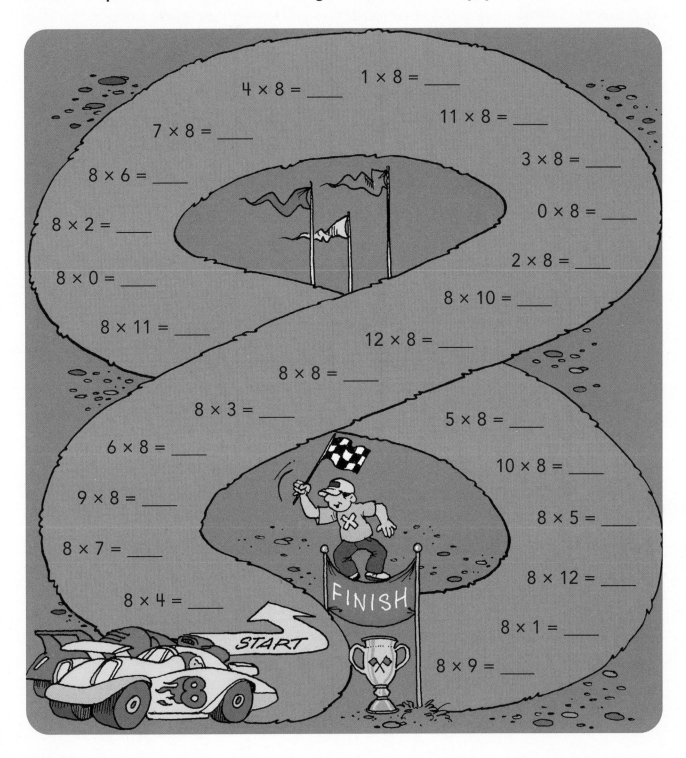

$4 \times 8 =$ _____

$1 \times 8 =$ _____

$7 \times 8 =$ _____

$11 \times 8 =$ _____

$8 \times 6 =$ _____

$3 \times 8 =$ _____

$8 \times 2 =$ _____

$0 \times 8 =$ _____

$8 \times 0 =$ _____

$2 \times 8 =$ _____

$8 \times 11 =$ _____

$8 \times 10 =$ _____

$12 \times 8 =$ _____

$8 \times 8 =$ _____

$8 \times 3 =$ _____

$5 \times 8 =$ _____

$6 \times 8 =$ _____

$10 \times 8 =$ _____

$9 \times 8 =$ _____

$8 \times 5 =$ _____

$8 \times 7 =$ _____

$8 \times 12 =$ _____

$8 \times 4 =$ _____

$8 \times 1 =$ _____

$8 \times 9 =$ _____

START

FINISH

A Product Search

Multiply. Then, circle the number word for each product in the puzzle. The words will go forward, backward, up, down, and diagonally. Be careful; some products appear more than once!

1 8 × 8 = _____   4 × 8 = _____   8 × 4 = _____   10 × 8 = _____

2 0 × 8 = _____   5 × 8 = _____   8 × 6 = _____   9 × 8 = _____

3 8 × 7 = _____   8 × 3 = _____   2 × 8 = _____   11 × 8 = _____

4 1 × 8 = _____   8 × 12 = _____   3 × 8 = _____   6 × 8 = _____

5 8 × 5 = _____   8 × 8 = _____   8 × 0 = _____

```
F  C  E  L  I  M  R  U  O  F  -  Y  T  N  E  W  T
O  O  F  O  R  T  Y  -  E  I  G  H  T  I  F  E  H
R  N  I  S  I  X  C  B  I  F  N  E  E  T  X  I  S
T  S  F  I  J  W  E  I  G  H  T  S  T  S  O  G  I
Y  I  T  X  T  F  H  R  H  S  Z  E  R  O  W  H  L
-  O  Y  T  W  V  O  S  T  I  U  V  W  V  T  T  R
E  W  -  E  E  U  I  R  Y  X  B  E  X  Y  -  Y  U
I  T  S  E  N  S  M  L  T  T  C  N  A  Z  Y  -  O
G  -  I  N  T  H  I  R  T  Y  -  T  W  O  T  E  F
H  Y  X  X  Y  Z  N  P  Q  -  D  Y  J  N  N  I  -
T  T  Y  Y  -  T  E  R  A  F  E  -  F  Q  E  G  Y
H  R  D  T  F  D  U  R  Z  O  G  T  K  O  V  H  T
G  I  H  R  O  F  V  Y  O  U  F  W  L  U  E  T  X
I  H  Y  O  U  E  W  X  C  R  H  O  M  W  S  T  I
E  T  L  F  R  N  I  N  E  T  Y  -  S  I  X  Z  S
```

Is There a Pattern?

Is there a pattern of the products when multiplying by 9? Yes! The sum of each product equals 9! There are two exceptions. One exception is 11 × 9 = 99; then each number in the product is 9! What is the other exception?

0 × 9 =		0
1 × 9 =		9
2 × 9 =	1	8
3 × 9 =	2	7
4 × 9 =	3	6
5 × 9 =	4	5
6 × 9 =	5	4
7 × 9 =	6	3
8 × 9 =	7	2
9 × 9 =	8	1
10 × 9 =	9	0

There seems to be a pattern here.

Unscramble the number word for each product of the following 9s multiplication facts. Then, write the 9s fact next to the number word.

1. ENO DDHNUER TEHGI _____

2. NYTENI-NNEI _____

3. TINENY _____

4. YITHEG-NOE _____

5. EENTVSY-WOT _____

6. YXTIS-ERETH _____

7. TFFIY-RUOF _____

8. YTRFO-EVIF _____

9. YHRTTI-XIS _____

Cross-Number Puzzle

Multiply. Write the number word for each product in the puzzle. Don't forget the hyphens! The first one is done for you.

Across

1. 9 × 5 = __45__

5. 1 × 9 = _____

7. 9 × 12 = _____

9. 4 × 9 = _____

10. 9 × 10 = _____

12. 2 × 9 = _____

13. 9 × 11 = _____

Down

2. 9 × 3 = _____

3. 6 × 9 = _____

4. 0 × 9 = _____

6. 9 × 8 = _____

8. 7 × 9 = _____

11. 9 × 9 = _____

Justin just finished putting together a puzzle of a castle and wants to know how many pieces are in the puzzle. He knows he put together 9 pieces every 5 minutes. If Justin worked for 1 hour, how many pieces does the puzzle have? Show your work on another sheet of paper.

Geometric Multiplication

Multiply. Color each triangle with an even product orange.
Color each triangle with an odd product blue.

8 × 6 = _____	9 × 4 = _____	8 × 9 = _____	8 × 12 = _____
7 × 9 = _____	7 × 7 = _____	9 × 3 = _____	9 × 11 = _____
7 × 7 = _____	4 × 6 = _____	8 × 7 = _____	1 × 7 = _____
8 × 8 = _____	9 × 5 = _____	5 × 7 = _____	8 × 10 = _____
6 × 9 = _____	9 × 9 = _____	7 × 3 = _____	6 × 6 = _____
7 × 11 = _____	5 × 8 = _____	6 × 3 = _____	9 × 7 = _____
1 × 9 = _____	5 × 9 = _____	7 × 5 = _____	3 × 9 = _____
7 × 10 = _____	7 × 6 = _____	9 × 8 = _____	6 × 12 = _____

Up, Up, and Away

Color each box that contains a multiplication sentence that is correct. Cross out each incorrect product and write the correct product.

$9 \times 12 = 108$

$7 \times 7 = 47$

$9 \times 5 = 95$

$6 \times 6 = 36$

$8 \times 9 = 79$

$9 \times 9 = 89$

$7 \times 11 = 77$

$3 \times 6 = 18$

$8 \times 4 = 32$

$8 \times 12 = 92$

$9 \times 3 = 27$

$12 \times 6 = 73$

$9 \times 10 = 19$

$6 \times 7 = 72$

$11 \times 8 = 81$

$7 \times 8 = 56$

$6 \times 9 = 54$

$8 \times 5 = 45$

$3 \times 7 = 21$

$7 \times 0 = 0$

A Learning Lesson

What's the best way to learn multiplication?

To find out, multiply. Then, use the code to write the letter of each multiplication sentence on the blank above its product.

A $1 \times 6 =$	**G** $4 \times 4 =$	**M** $6 \times 12 =$	**S** $9 \times 3 =$
C $5 \times 9 =$	**H** $8 \times 8 =$	**N** $7 \times 7 =$	**T** $8 \times 12 =$
D $7 \times 8 =$	**I** $10 \times 9 =$	**O** $2 \times 6 =$	**U** $9 \times 9 =$
E $5 \times 5 =$	**K** $3 \times 12 =$	**P** $9 \times 2 =$	**Y** $9 \times 12 =$
F $4 \times 6 =$	**L** $7 \times 12 =$	**R** $12 \times 5 =$	**!** $0 \times 3 =$

___ ___ ___ ___   ___ ___ ___   ___ ___ ___ ___ ___
24 90 49 56   96 64 25   60 90 16 64 96

___ ___ ___ ___ ___ ___ ___ ___ ,   ___ ___ ___
18 60 12 56 81 45 96 27   16 25 96

___ ___ ___ ___   ___ ___   ___ ___ ___ ___ ___
96 64 25 72   96 12   27 96 90 45 36

___ ___   ___ ___ ___ ___   ___ ___ ___ ___ ,
90 49   108 12 81 60   64 25 6 56

,

___ ___ ___   ___ ___ ___ ___   ___ ___ ___
6 49 56   56 12 49 96   84 25 96

___ ___ ___ ___   ___ ___ ___ ___ ___ ___ ___
96 64 25 72   25 27 45 6 18 25 0

Around Town

Multiply.

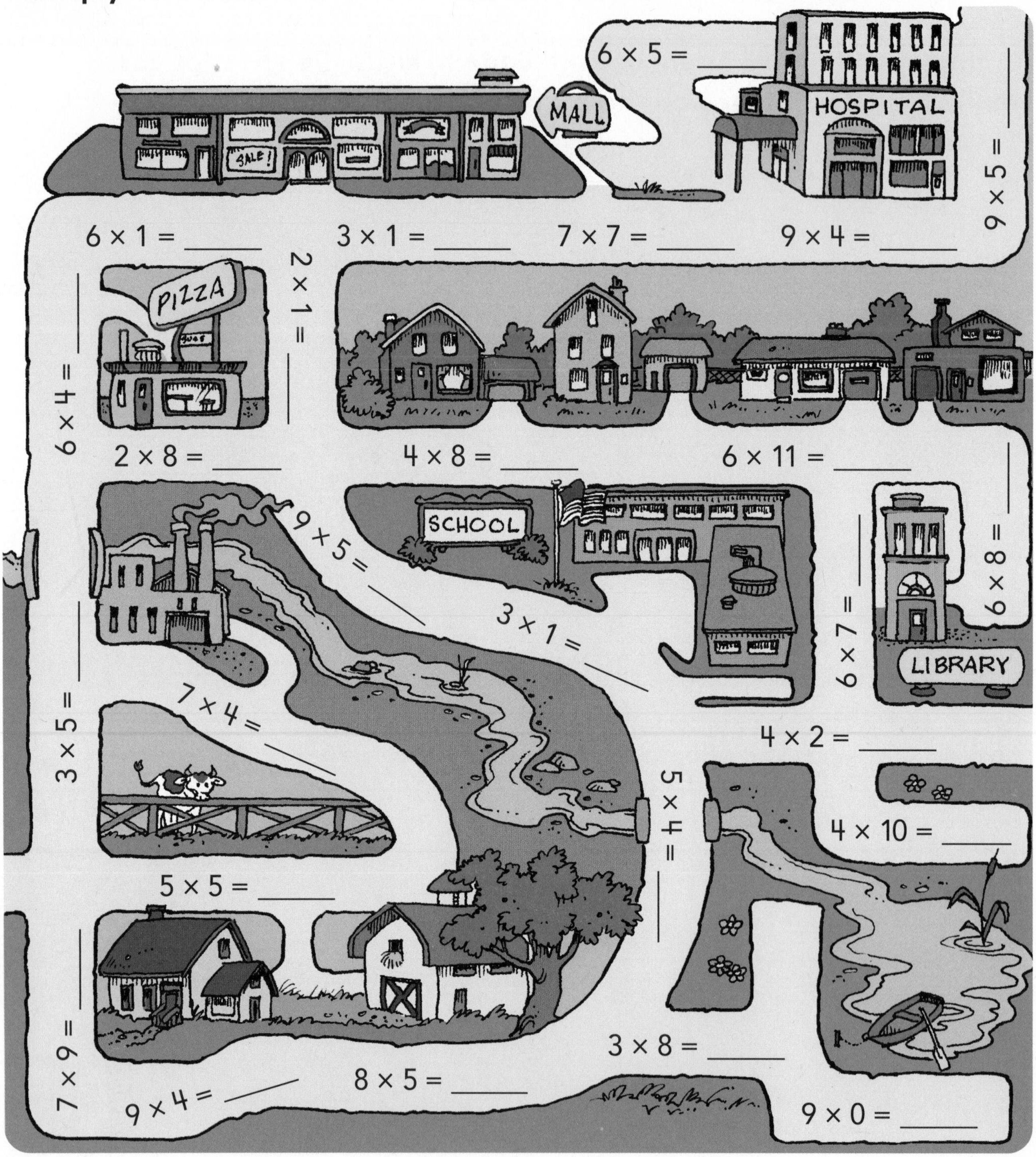

6 × 5 = ____
MALL
HOSPITAL
SALE!
9 × 5 = ____
6 × 1 = ____
3 × 1 = ____
7 × 7 = ____
9 × 4 = ____
PIZZA
2 × 1 = ____
6 × 4 = ____
2 × 8 = ____
4 × 8 = ____
6 × 11 = ____
SCHOOL
9 × 5 = ____
3 × 1 = ____
6 × 7 = ____
6 × 8 = ____
LIBRARY
3 × 5 = ____
7 × 4 = ____
4 × 2 = ____
5 × 4 = ____
4 × 10 = ____
5 × 5 = ____
7 × 9 = ____
3 × 8 = ____
9 × 4 = ____
8 × 5 = ____
9 × 0 = ____

Dot-to-Dot Multiplication

If you wanted to travel to Multiplication Island, what would be the most exciting way to get there?

To find out, multiply. Then, connect the dots in order from 10 to 42.

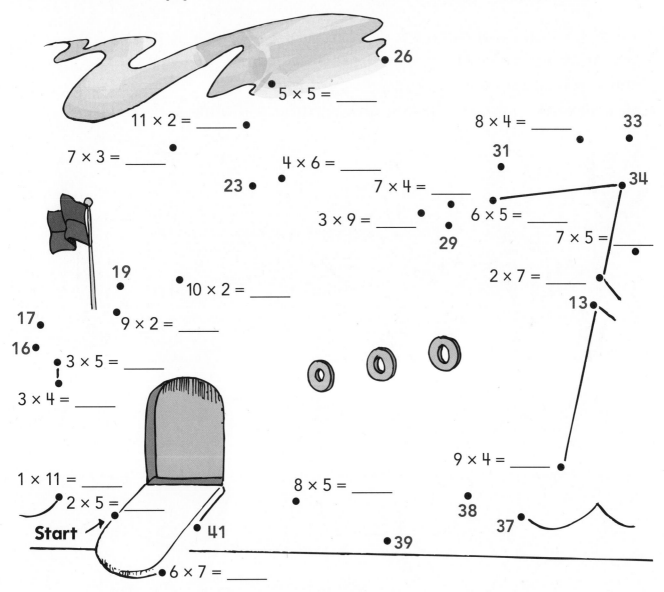

• 26

$5 \times 5 =$ _____

$11 \times 2 =$ _____ •

$7 \times 3 =$ _____ •

$4 \times 6 =$ _____

23 •

$7 \times 4 =$ _____

$8 \times 4 =$ _____ **33**

31

34

$3 \times 9 =$ _____ • $6 \times 5 =$ _____

29

$7 \times 5 =$ _____

$2 \times 7 =$ _____

13 •

19

$10 \times 2 =$ _____

17 •

$9 \times 2 =$ _____

16 •

$3 \times 5 =$ _____

$3 \times 4 =$ _____

$9 \times 4 =$ _____

$1 \times 11 =$ _____

$2 \times 5 =$ _____

Start

$8 \times 5 =$ _____

41

38

37

• **39**

$6 \times 7 =$ _____

One day Max discovered 7 banana plants and 5 coconut palm trees. He picked 6 bananas from each banana plant and 4 coconuts from each coconut palm tree. On another sheet of paper, find out how many total bananas and how many total coconuts Max picked.

The "Ten" Flower

Multiplying by 10 is really easy! Multiply the factor by 1 and add a 0.

10 × 8 = _____ (Multiply 1 × 8 = 8, and add a 0. The product is 80.)

10 × 12 = _____ (Multiply 1 × 12 = 12, and add a 0. The product is 120.)

Multiply. Then, color each space with a product less than 50 red.

Color each space with a product greater than 70 orange.

Color each space with a product equal to 50 yellow.

Color all other spaces with a multiplication sentence green.

Cloud Ten

When multiplying by 10, the product always ends in 0.

Multiply.

10 × 8 = _____

10 × 9 = _____

10 × 0 = _____

1 × 10 = _____

3 × 10 = _____

10 × 5 = _____

10 × 2 = _____

7 × 10 = _____

9 × 10 = _____

6 × 10 = _____

8 × 10 = _____

10 × 3 = _____

10 × 11 = _____

HANG TEN!

10 × 4 = _____

10 × 10 = _____

2 × 10 = _____

10 × 7 = _____

0 × 10 = _____

10 × 1 = _____

COOL!

10 × 10 = _____

11 × 10 = _____

4 × 10 = _____

10 × 6 = _____

10 × 12 = _____

12 × 10 = _____

5 × 10 = _____

Every morning Miranda chose her favorite 10 clouds in the sky. She especially liked clouds that looked like animals. If Miranda did this every morning for a week, how many clouds would she choose altogether? Show your work on another sheet of paper.

Eleven! Eleven!

Look at each multiplication sentence. If the product is correct, circle it. If the product is incorrect, cross it out and write the correct product above it.

When multiplying the factor 11 by a number from 1 to 9, double the number to find the product. Examples:
11 × 5 = 55
11 × 7 = 77

8 × 11 = 81

3 × 11 = 33

4 × 11 = 48

5 × 11 = 66

9 × 11 = 99

11 × 6 = 66

2 × 11 = 22

7 × 11 = 74

6 × 11 = 54

11 × 3 = 23

11 × 8 = 88

11 × 5 = 55

1 × 1 = 12

11 × 2 = 21

FINE DINING

11 × 4 = 44

11 × 9 = 88

11 × 1 = 11

The "Tuffys"

Multiply. If the multiplication sentence is a "tuffy," color the space blue. If it is a double, color the space yellow.

The rest of the multiplication facts with a factor of 11 are: $11 \times 0 = 0$, $11 \times 10 = 110$, $11 \times 11 = 121$, and $11 \times 12 = 132$. Since you cannot just double the number being multiplied by 11, these are the "tuffys."

$11 \times 12 =$ _____

$12 \times 11 =$ _____

$11 \times 10 =$ _____

$10 \times 11 =$ _____

$11 \times 1 =$ _____

$1 \times 11 =$ _____

$11 \times 8 =$ _____

$8 \times 11 =$ _____

$11 \times 6 =$ _____

$6 \times 11 =$ _____

$11 \times 10 =$ _____

$10 \times 11 =$ _____

$11 \times 4 =$ _____

$4 \times 11 =$ _____

$11 \times 3 =$ _____

$3 \times 11 =$ _____

$11 \times 9 =$ _____

$9 \times 11 =$ _____

$11 \times 7 =$ _____

$7 \times 11 =$ _____

$11 \times 0 =$ _____

$0 \times 11 =$ _____

$11 \times 2 =$ _____

$2 \times 11 =$ _____

$11 \times 11 =$ _____

$11 \times 12 =$ _____

$12 \times 11 =$ _____

$11 \times 5 =$ _____

$5 \times 11 =$ _____

Searching for Facts of Twelve

Multiply. Then, circle the number word for each product in the puzzle. The words will go across, down, and diagonally.

1 12 × 0 = _____   12 × 4 = _____   12 × 7 = _____   12 × 10 = _____

2 12 × 1 = _____   12 × 5 = _____   12 × 8 = _____   12 × 11 = _____

3 12 × 2 = _____   12 × 6 = _____   12 × 9 = _____   12 × 12 = _____

4 12 × 3 = _____

```
O N E H U N D R E R T H I R T Y - T W O
R N F X W F R Q R I P D B Q E H B H O P
E Q E Z T O O U C Z G S C I O D M I A F
O N E H U N D R E D E I G H T R T R T O
Y W I L U I G U N N R X D W L E N H Y R
M T E N V N H W T H I R T Y - S I X G T
E W F O N E D U K D L E A T R E B C Y Y
T E G N E T R R O H U T T D X E E O P -
Y N O H S Y H H E I G H T Y - F O U R E
P T I U E - G V B D H I D W N Q J N T I
L Y W N X S L I E E T R J F E I G H Y G
D - T H V I O W S N Y W J K F L B T N H
A F T S I X T Y O E T X E K O L V C K T
K O U G E U Y R E N I Y O N R Y V E T Z
T U R H U V D D Z S E V E N T Y - T W O
F R E S O N E F T E T Y F I X Y A Y E C
A N T F V U R N O R R M S O U T Y I R J
O N E H U N D R E D F O R T Y - F O U R
```

Thinking Thoughts of Twelve

Write a multiplication fact in each box using 12 as a factor for the product on each wastebasket. Use a different sentence for each product.

1. 84   0

2. 96   132   72   144   36

3. 12   60   84   108   48

4. 120   48   96   132   24

There Are No Obstacles Too Big for You!

Use a stopwatch to time how long it takes to multiply around the obstacle course.

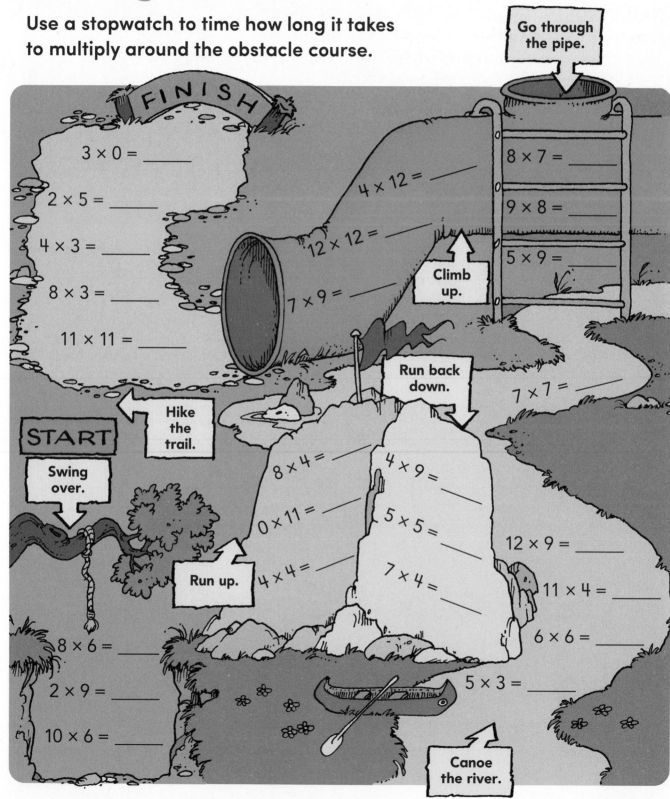

Go through the pipe.

$8 \times 7 =$ _____

$9 \times 8 =$ _____

$5 \times 9 =$ _____

Climb up.

$4 \times 12 =$ _____

$12 \times 12 =$ _____

$7 \times 9 =$ _____

$3 \times 0 =$ _____

$2 \times 5 =$ _____

$4 \times 3 =$ _____

$8 \times 3 =$ _____

$11 \times 11 =$ _____

Hike the trail.

Run back down.

$7 \times 7 =$ _____

START

Swing over.

Run up.

$8 \times 4 =$ _____

$0 \times 11 =$ _____

$4 \times 4 =$ _____

$4 \times 9 =$ _____

$5 \times 5 =$ _____

$7 \times 4 =$ _____

$12 \times 9 =$ _____

$11 \times 4 =$ _____

$6 \times 6 =$ _____

$5 \times 3 =$ _____

$8 \times 6 =$ _____

$2 \times 9 =$ _____

$10 \times 6 =$ _____

Canoe the river.

Multiplication Success

Why are multiplicationists so successful?

To find out, multiply. Then, use the code to write the letter of each multiplication sentence on the blank above its product.

A $10 \times 10 =$	**G** $3 \times 1 =$	**N** $12 \times 8 =$	**S** $6 \times 9 =$
B $6 \times 7 =$	**H** $9 \times 9 =$	**O** $6 \times 6 =$	**T** $6 \times 0 =$
C $5 \times 6 =$	**I** $8 \times 9 =$	**P** $11 \times 12 =$	**U** $5 \times 8 =$
E $7 \times 7 =$	**L** $12 \times 2 =$	**Q** $8 \times 8 =$	**V** $7 \times 3 =$
F $3 \times 9 =$	**M** $3 \times 6 =$	**R** $4 \times 5 =$	**Y** $2 \times 8 =$

49 21 49 20 16   132 20 36 42 24 49 18

0 81 49 16   49 96 30 36 40 96 0 49 20   72 96

24 72 27 49   42 49 30 36 18 49 54   100

30 81 100 24 24 49 96 3 49 0 36

30 36 96 64 40 49 20 !

   Scholastic Success With Multiplication Facts • Grades 3–4   **45**

ANSWER KEY

Page 5
1. 2 × 3 = 6 **2.** 3 × 3 = 9 **3.** 4 × 2 = 8
4. 3 × 5 = 15 **5.** 1 × 3 = 3 **6.** 4 × 3 = 12
7. 2 × 6 = 12 **8.** 3 × 4 = 12 **9.** 3 × 6 = 18
10. 5 × 3 = 15 **11.** 5 × 1 = 5 **12.** 7 × 2 = 14
13. 3 × 2 = 6 **14.** 2 × 4 = 8
15. 4 × 7 = 28 **16.** 4 × 5 = 20

Page 6
1. 2 × 4 = 8 **2.** 3 × 3 = 9 **3.** 3 × 5 = 15
4. 4 × 3 = 12 **5.** 4 × 1 = 4 **6.** 6 × 3 = 18
7. 8 × 2 = 16 **8.** 6 × 4 = 24
9. 2 × 6 = 12 **10.** 8 × 3 = 24
11. 3 × 6 = 18 **12.** 4 × 5 = 20
13. 2 × 2 = 4 **14.** 6 × 1 = 6
15. 5 × 4 = 20 **16.** 7 × 2 = 14
Extra Activity: Check diagram.
5 × 7 = 35 oranges

Page 7
1. 3 × 5 = 15 **2.** 4 × 6 = 24 **3.** 2 × 8 = 16
4. 4 × 2 = 8 **5.** 3 × 7 = 21 **6.** 4 × 4 = 16
7. 3 × 9 = 27 **8.** 5 × 5 = 25 **9.** 5 × 3 = 15
10. 4 × 10 = 40 **11.** 5 × 1 = 5 **12.** 3 × 11 = 33
13. 4 × 8 = 32 **14.** 4 × 0 = 0
15. 4 × 12 = 48 **16.** 4 × 9 = 36

Page 8
1. 4 × 4 = 16 **2.** 7 × 2 = 14 **3.** 2 × 5 = 10
4. 4 × 5 = 20 **5.** 3 × 7 = 21 **6.** 6 × 2 = 12
7. 8 × 3 = 24 **8.** 9 × 1 = 9

Page 9
1. 2 × 6 = 12 **2.** 9 × 3 = 27
3. 9 × 5 = 45 **4.** 4 × 7 = 28
5. 8 × 9 = 72 **6.** 10 × 4 = 40
7. 11 × 2 = 22 **8.** 8 × 4 = 32
9. 7 × 3 = 21 **10.** 7 × 6 = 42
11. 12 × 3 = 36 **12.** 5 × 6 = 30
13. 7 × 9 = 63 **14.** 11 × 12 = 132

Page 10
1. 2 × 3 = 6, 3 × 2 = 6, 6 ÷ 2 = 3,
6 ÷ 3 = 2 **2.** 3 × 5 = 15, 5 × 3 = 15,
15 ÷ 3 = 5, 15 ÷ 5 = 3 **3.** 5 × 6 = 30,
6 × 5 = 30, 30 ÷ 5 = 6, 30 ÷ 6 = 5
4. 2 × 8 = 16, 8 × 2 = 16, 16 ÷ 2 = 8,
16 ÷ 8 = 2 **5.** 3 × 9 = 27, 9 × 3 = 27,
27 ÷ 3 = 9, 27 ÷ 9 = 3 **6.** 6 × 7 = 42,
7 × 6 = 42, 42 ÷ 6 = 7, 42 ÷ 7 = 6
7. 4 × 5 = 20, 5 × 4 = 20, 20 ÷ 4 = 5,
20 ÷ 5 = 4 **8.** 3 × 12 = 36, 12 × 3 = 36,
36 ÷ 3 = 12, 36 ÷ 12 = 3 **9.** 4 × 8 = 32,
8 × 4 = 32, 32 ÷ 4 = 8, 32 ÷ 8 = 4
Extra Activity: 33 ÷ 3 = 11 marbles
3, 11, 33

Page 11
Check grids. **1.** (3, 4), 12 **2.** (2, 4), 8
3. (3, 2), 6 **4.** (1, 5), 5 **5.** (5, 2), 10
6. (3, 6), 18

Page 12
1. 15, 18, 21, 24, 27 **2.** 20, 24, 28, 32, 36
3. 5, 6, 7, 8, 9 **4.** 28, 35, 42, 49, 56
5. 40, 50, 60, 70, 80 **6.** 9, 36, 45, 54, 63
7. 18, 24, 36, 42, 48 **8.** 11, 33, 55, 66, 77
9. 20, 25, 30, 35, 40 **10.** 16, 32, 48,
56, 64 **11.** 16, 18, 20, 24, 26
12. 12, 36, 72, 84, 96, 108

Page 13
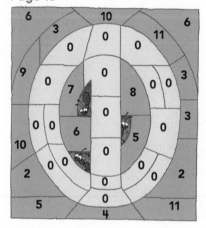

Page 14
1. 6, 16, 22, 14 **2.** 16, 8, 4, 8 **3.** 24, 10,
20, 24 **4.** 18, 2, 20, 14 **5.** 0, 12, 6, 0
6. 10, 18 **7.** 12, 2 **8.** 22, 4
Extra Activity: Rhymes will vary.

Page 15
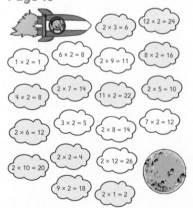

Page 16

Page 17

Page 18
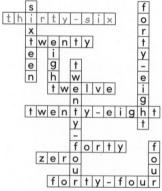

Extra Activity: 44 buttons

Page 19
A. 40 **D.** 16 **E.** 44 **I.** 0 **M.** 8 **N.** 20
O. 28 **R.** 24 **S.** 12 **T.** 32 **Y.** 36 **!.** 48
YES! I ADORE IT MORE AND MORE!
Extra Activity: Check message.

Page 20

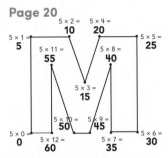

$5 \times 2 = $ **10** $5 \times 4 = $ **20**
$5 \times 1 = $ **5** $5 \times 5 = $ **25**
$5 \times 11 = $ **55** $5 \times 8 = $ **40**
$5 \times 3 = $ **15**
$5 \times 0 = $ **0** $5 \times 10 = $ **50** $5 \times 9 = $ **45** $5 \times 6 = $ **30**
$5 \times 12 = $ **60** $5 \times 7 = $ **35**

Extra Activity: 15 scoops

Page 21

1. 10 **2.** 1 **3.** 7 **4.** 50 **5.** 12
6. 30 **7.** 11 **8.** 15 **9.** 40 **10.** 9
11. 5 **12.** 5 **13.** 35 **14.** 60 **15.** 4
Extra Activity: 48 nuts

Page 22

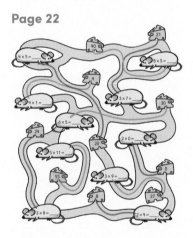

Page 23

A. 36 **B.** 50 **D.** 16 **E.** 44 **G.** 12 **H.** 18
I. 28 **L.** 30 **M.** 32 **N.** 27 **O.** 21 **P.** 0 **R.** 22
S. 35 **T.** 45 **U.** 24 **W.** 25 **Y.** 48 **!.** 9
**SO THAT HIS GROUP WOULD BEGIN
TO GET LARGER AND MULTIPLY!**
Extra Activity: Mr. Weaver's class has
24 students. Ms. Vega's class has 20
students. Mr. Weaver''s class has more
students.

Page 24

A. 22 **B.** 7 **C.** 18 **D.** 48 **E.** 36 **G.** 16
H. 60 **I.** 12 **M.** 44 **O.** 21 **P.** 40 **R.** 30
S. 45 **T.** 35 **U.** 28 **V.** 33 **Y.** 24 **!.** 0
**BECAUSE YOU HAVE THE RIGHT
PRODUCT EVERY TIME!**

Page 25

yellow: 0 + 66 + 12 + 60 = 138
red: 18 + 30 + 36 + 6 + 24 = 114
orange: 54 + 18 + 66 + 24 + 30 + 48 = 240
blue: 42 + 72 + 60 + 24 = 198
green: 30 + 42 + 48 + 72 + 0 = 192
purple: 36 + 24 + 12 + 18 + 6 = 96
Extra Activity: 48 fireworks

Page 26

1. 3 × 6 = 18 **2.** 6 × 5 = 30
3. 9 × 6 = 54 **4.** 11 × 6 = 66
5. 6 × 2 = 12 **6.** 4 × 6 = 24
7. 8 × 6 = 48 **8.** 7 × 6 = 42
9. 6 × 12 = 72 **10.** 0 × 6 = 0
11. 1 × 6 = 6 **12.** 10 × 6 = 60
1. 30, ★×◇= ◔★ **2.** 42, ◔×◆= ▱▪
3. 54, ◔×⬠= ★▱ **4.** 18, ◔×◔= ◔▲
5. 48, ◔×▲= ▱▲ **6.** 36, ◔×◔= ⬡
7. 72, ✚×◔= ◆▪ **8.** 60, ◔×☾= ◔★
Extra Activity: 72 flower symbols

Page 27

Extra Activity: 42 months; no

Page 28

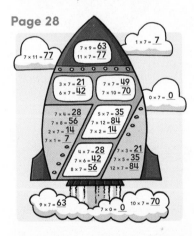

Page 29

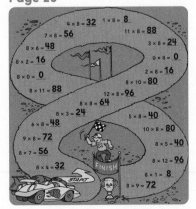

Page 30

1. 16, 32, 32, 80 **2.** 0, 40, 48, 72
3. 56, 24, 16, 88 **4.** 8, 96, 24, 48
5. 40, 64, 0

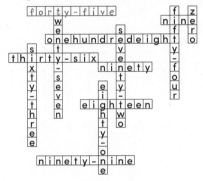

Page 31

The other exception is 0 × 9 = 0.
1. one hundred eight, 12 × 9 = 108
2. ninety-nine, 11 × 9 = 99
3. ninety, 10 × 9 = 90
4. eighty-one, 9 × 9 = 81
5. seventy-two, 8 × 9 = 72
6. sixty-three, 7 × 9 = 63
7. fifty-four, 6 × 9 = 54
8. forty-five, 5 × 9 = 45
9. thirty-six, 4 × 9 = 36

Page 32

forty-five / zero / nine / fifty-four / one hundred eight / thirty-six / ninety / seventy-two / eighteen / ninety-nine / sixty-seven / sixty-three / eighty-one (crossword)

Extra Activity: 108 pieces

Page 33

48	36	72	96
63	49	27	99
49	24	56	7
64	45	35	80
54	81	21	36
77	40	18	63
9	45	35	27
70	42	72	72

Page 34

9 × 12 = 108
7 × 7 = 49
8 × 9 = 72
9 × 5 = 45
6 × 6 = 36
9 × 9 = 81
7 × 11 = 77
3 × 6 = 18
8 × 4 = 32
8 × 12 = 96
9 × 3 = 27
12 × 6 = 72
9 × 10 = 90
6 × 7 = 42
11 × 8 = 88
7 × 8 = 56
6 × 9 = 54
8 × 5 = 40
3 × 7 = 21
7 × 0 = 0

Page 35

A. 6 **C.** 45 **D.** 56 **E.** 25 **F.** 24 **G.** 16
H. 64 **I.** 90 **K.** 36 **L.** 84 **M.** 72 **N.** 49
O. 12 **P.** 18 **R.** 60 **S.** 27 **T.** 96 **U.** 81
Y. 108 **!.** 0
**FIND THE RIGHT PRODUCTS, GET
THEM TO STICK IN YOUR HEAD, AND
DON'T LET THEM ESCAPE!**

Page 36

Page 37

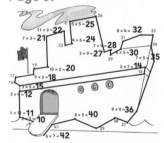

Extra Activity: 42 bananas, 20 coconuts

Page 38

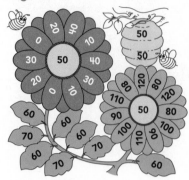

Page 39

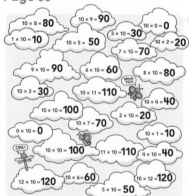

Extra Activity: 70 clouds

Page 40

Page 41

Page 42

1. 0, 48, 84, 120; **2.** 12, 60, 96, 121;
3. 24, 72, 108, 144; **4.** 36

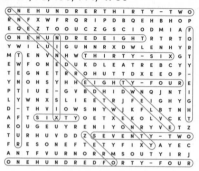

Page 43

1. 12 × 7 = 84, 12 × 0 = 0
2. 12 × 8 = 96, 12 × 11 = 132,
12 × 6 = 72, 12 × 12 = 144, 12 × 3 = 36
3. 12 × 1 = 12, 12 × 5 = 60,
7 × 12 = 84, 12 × 9 = 108, 12 × 4 = 48
4. 12 × 10 = 120, 4 × 12 = 48,
8 × 12 = 96, 11 × 12 = 132, 2 × 12 = 24

Page 44

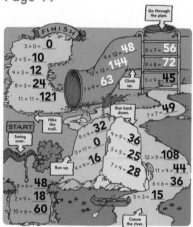

Page 45

A. 100 **B.** 42 **C.** 30 **E.** 49 **F.** 27 **G.** 3
H. 81 **I.** 72 **L.** 24 **M.** 18 **N.** 96 **O.** 36
P. 132 **Q.** 64 **R.** 20 **S.** 54 **T.** 0 **U.** 40
V. 21 **Y.** 16
**EVERY PROBLEM THEY ENCOUNTER
IN LIFE BECOMES A CHALLENGE TO
CONQUER!**